The CEO's Little Black Book of Leadership Communications

The CEO's Little Black Book of Leadership Communications

Granville Toogood

Dedication

For my children and grandchildren: Heather and Wayne, Carolyn and Chase, Gigi, Sharkey, Tally Man, Gray Man, Heath Bar Crunch and Pippa. And a special tribute to my wife of 40 years, Patricia.

Table of Contents

Chapter One . . . . . The Perfect Presentation   1

- Custom design it
- How to fly it
- Why it matters
- The Power Formula
- The Foundation
- How to command any stage or conference room

Chapter Two . . . . . Selling Product or Service   21

- The smart approach
- The Waffle and The Wafer
- New rules for visual aids and presentation books
- New rules for business presentations
- New rules for financial services presentations

Chapter Three . . . Reporting Up   33

- Winning with the unexpected
- Breaking bad habits
- Overcoming cultural objections
- New rules about information vs. knowledge

Chapter Four . . . . Mastering PowerPoint   45

- Creating smart visual aids that work for
  you—not against you
- New rules for pictures and graphs
- Command and control

Chapter Five . . . . Prepared Text   53

- Speak like a pro—even with no preparation
- New rules for the podium
- Your ultimate safety net

Think About It

When Paul Newman gets whacked to the ground in "Cool Hand Luke," the chain gang boss looms over the dazed con and casually observes, "What we have here is a failure to communicate…"

In the movie, Newman's disconnect with the chain gang boss and his inability to express himself nearly costs him his life.

In business, a failure to communicate can cost jobs and money. When Treasury Secretary Hank Paulson failed to convince Congress of the inseparable connection between Wall Street and Main Street the whole historical rescue package of 2008 almost derailed, and for a breathless few days the economy of the entire world hung in the balance.

When Wall Street hired nuclear physicists and math PhDs to design exotic new financial instruments, the bankers were unable to comprehend the complexities of the very products they were selling—because they had no idea what the egg-heads were talking about. The resulting flood of mortgage backed securities and other dubious derivatives brought the nation to the brink of financial catastrophe, crushed global markets and destroyed trillions of dollars in wealth.

When scientists from the Xerox Research Lab in California failed to persuade the suits in Rochester of the value of computers and what would later become the Internet, Xerox missed the biggest business opportunity in history.

In politics and in business a talent for persuasion and articulation can mean the difference between stunning success and even more spectacular failure.

The risk of being ill equipped to compete is simply not an option.

That's why today more than ever we have all got to be prepared to inspire employees, customers, peers, managements, investors and lots of other very important people who ultimately make the decisions that determine our lives.

Think about what's happening.

After years of relative calm and prosperity, we now find ourselves in times of unprecedented turmoil and reinvention. Not since the 1930s have Americans experienced such sweeping change and challenge. With seismic economic events and their backlash sweeping the globe, people everywhere are discovering that they can no longer depend on traditional market and business models. Economic structures that we've known and trusted for generations are threatening to come unglued, and it is taking all of our powers and resources to keep them intact. At the same time, iconic institutions are toppling.

In a reversal many pundits never thought they would see in their lifetime, the private sector is morphing into the public sector and the public sector is morphing into the private sector.

All of this upset presents a brand new challenge to business leaders, executives, managers and entrepreneurs, who are beginning to realize they have no choice but to dig deep into their own natural talents, creativity and ingenuity to navigate a new and unfamiliar landscape rich with peril and opportunity.

For the agile few, this kind of unpredictable, less stable, more chaotic environment can be a very good thing. But for the fragile it can be a time of uncertainty and trepidation.

We all feel like we could use some help—and that's what this little book is all about.

By now, you may understand only too clearly that your future really is in your own hands.

It will be up to YOU to position yourself (and your company) as leaders in your industry. It will be up to YOU to sell yourself and create action, to inspire employees to higher performance, win customers, drive teams, enlist managements and peers, influence investors, move service or product, get elected to office, or even to get new job. It will be up to YOU to take charge of your fortunes and probe your possibilities and limits.

No one else is going to help you, or do these things for you.

So into your hands I extend not only a kind of life vest to keep you above water, but also a universal pocket tool to success, even under duress.

In these pages you will find a quick synopsis of some of the coaching and advice I have given to more than half the Fortune 500 CEOs, political candidates, executives, public figures, global business leaders and celebrities over the past quarter century. And as you will see, it's all based on just three simple propositions:

1. Three minutes with the right audience can be worth more than a year at your desk.

2. Talent and brainpower alone can not guarantee success.

3. Conversations are far more effective than presentations.

The daunting challenges and changes we see around us demand personal action and sharper leadership. But if that weren't enough, you may already have read results of recent research which reveals that business leaders the world over value leadership communications ABOVE ALL OTHER BUSINESS SKILLS.

Jack Welch, the former CEO of General Electric, says that if you are in business today, one of your first jobs is to what he calls, OVERCOMMUNICATE. In other words, Welch says YOU CAN NEVER COMMUNICATE ENOUGH—firing up your own people, getting closer to customers, keeping investors posted on every development. Where are you going? Why? What are you doing to get there? Employees and investors particularly need to know. Welch says a failure to over communicate could cost you your job or your business. By contrast, a strategic decision to over communicate could propel you ahead of everyone else.

So the idea here is to give you the knowledge you will need to command any sale, stage, podium or conference room, and compel any audience to do your bidding, gets things done, or simply say yes. When you acquire, then begin to master, these surprisingly easy-to -learn skills, you can eclipse peers and competitors and vault yourself, and career, almost overnight to another level.

You should be able to put these principles to work immediately, with measurable positive rewards to follow.

To begin, let's take a look at what constitutes the perfect "presentation"…

Chapter 1

The Perfect Presentation— Architecture

First of all, I don't want to talk about presentations. I don't like presentations. (I'll bet you don't, either). Presentations for the most part are boring, and we certainly don't want to bore. Boredom doesn't say much for us, our product, or service—and it's not good for business.

So what to do?

Given a choice, would you rather sit through a presentation, or have a conversation? If you are like me, you would choose a conversation any day. But of course, as much as we'd like to, we can't really escape presentations. The fact is that people will always be giving presentations. But the solution to the boredom dilemma is easy.

We will disguise our "presentations" as conversations.

From now on, all your presentations will be so different, they will look and sound like enlarged conversations—even though you may be doing most of the talking.

And that's where The Perfect Presentation comes in. The Perfect Presentation automatically turns every presentation into a conversation.

The Perfect Pitch has only five parts:

1.	Strong start
2.	One theme
3.	Good examples
4.	Ordinary language
5.	Strong ending.

This as what I call the architecture.

Put the five parts of the architecture together and they become the POWER Formula:

P	Punch
O	One theme
W	Windows
E	Ear
R	Retention

P Punch.

Here are eight ways to begin strongly:

1.	Tell a personal story to make your business point.
2.	Use an anecdote, example or illustration to make your business point.
3.	Begin with the ending (the bottom line—your theme).
4.	Ask a rhetorical question.
5.	Use a quotation (business-related only).
6.	Project into the future.
7.	Look into the past.
8.	Humor (not recommended).

It's essential to have a strong beginning, because—

■ We don't want to violate what I call the 8-second rule. The 8-second rule says that subconsciously people decide within just 8 seconds whether we are worth listening to in the first place.

■ We want to capture the mind of the audience immediately.

■ We want to look—and sound—more professional and compelling than the next guy.

That means that opening amenities ("Good morning, it is a pleasure to be here today, etc….") have to go. Opening amenities are opening inanities. If necessary, they can stay—but only after a strong start. For example you can launch with a personal story, and then say, "…and that's why I want to thank our hosts and tell how you all how delighted to be here today, because I think we may have an opportunity now to resolve some of these kinds of issues before it is too late…"

My personal feeling is that you never need to bother with amenities. But if you must, then that's how you do it.

Given a choice, 99 percent of captive listeners would rather hear you tell a personal story than suffer through an opening amenity.

Personal story

Once you decide on your theme, you can tell a personal story to embrace that theme. Leaders have been using this intimate approach for millennia with good effect. The key is to match the story with the message. A personal story gets everyone involved immediately, opens an instant emotional connection between the speaker and the audience, and quickly reveals the theme in a way that bypasses the intellect and goes straight to the gut (to seize the intellect, first we must target the gut).

If you can, tell your story in under a minute.

For example, if your theme is the need for a rebirth of research and development in your corporate culture, you could say something like this:

"Two weeks ago I had a brief tour of a competitor in Japan that opened my eyes to a problem we've got to fix...the R&D facility was twice the size of their manufacturing facility with a budget three times or own R&D budget...which in my estimation puts them three years ahead in product pipeline with a four year head start in the marketplace...

"….And this is just one example of how our competitors are pulling out all the stops to develop new systems—while we seem to be going the other way...

"...But if we wake up and get serious once again about research and development, I see seven ways we can regain our lead in the marketplace—without incurring significant cost..."

Straight to the gut. A quick cautionary tale that grabs the theme, rings the alarm bell, presents a challenge and provides some hope—all in just a few seconds. They are with you heart and mind 100 percent. You are off to a fast start.

Tell an anecdote

Not a personal story, but a story about something you heard, saw, read, or somebody told you. This may be a little different from a personal story, but the effect is the same.

Example: "You might have read the story in the Financial Times the other day that said that if United States companies stop seeking short term gains at the expense of research and development, in just a few years America could once again lead markets worldwide and leave China and India wondering what hit them…."

Then you connect to your theme, build your case, start proving your point, and you're on your way. This time we are using a more positive approach. As you can see, an anecdote can be almost as compelling as a first-hand eyewitness personal story.

Begin with the ending

This approach is almost fail-safe. It not only gets right down to business without delay, but is also the simplest solution if you can't decide how to begin. Better yet, senior managers love it. Who will fault you for getting right to the point (as long as you continue on to press the case and prove your thesis)? Who will fault you for being three times more interesting, and memorable, while delivering more business value to the conversion in less than half the time?

Example: "My message is simple…The United States is close to a tripping point beyond which we will be unable to regain our pole position in global markets…But we still have a few precious years to double and triple our investment in

R&D—and reposition ourselves once again at the top of the pyramid…

"Here's what we've got to do…

"First…"

This is the kind of message you might want to bring, say, to an industry conference. In that case a straightforward approach has even more value, because your audience will probably have to listen to a half dozen or so other people, as well. Your listeners will be grateful to you for wasting no time and having right at it. Plus, they will be more likely to remember what you said and who you are.

Rhetorical question

You can count on an interesting rhetorical question to engage the mind.

Example: "I have just one question—What is single the thing about your business that keeps you up at night?.." (Pause)

"…I don't know about you…but what keeps me up at night is the knowledge that R&D in the U.S. is down more than 22 percent in the last five years, but up more than 500 percent in emerging market countries such as China, India, Brazil, Vietnam and South Africa…

"The good news is that some of our marquis companies such as General Electric and Boeing have already begun to recognize the problem and do something about it…and the momentum continues to build…."

Quotation

Quotations can backfire because they can be too pre-cious, and as a rule seem to draw more attention to the clever-ness of the speaker than the message. So avoid Aristophanes, Virgil and Tennyson. However, a relevant observation from the Fed Chairman might work just fine.

For example, "You may have read last week that the Fed-eral Reserve Chairman hinted that—quote—'Unprecedented oil and food prices and the dollar's new low against the Euro'—unquote—may lead to yet another downward rate adjust-ment...

"To me, this is just the latest wakeup call in a series of wakeup calls over the last 12 months that the window of oppor-tunity to regain our competitive edge is beginning to close..."

Then straight to your theme and call for action.

Project into the Future

In business, a forward-looking view is a benchmark of leadership. Managements value the man or woman who does not hesitate to venture a projection based on the best evidence of today. Business is not about where we have been, or where we are now, but where we are going. All knowledge about the past and present exists simply to serve the future—because that's where all the real action is.

Few people recognize this opportunity. Begin with the future in important meetings, and you will build a reputation as someone to watch. Beyond that, you will serve your audi-ence well.

Example: "Three years from now this business can be very different from the business we know today—for three reasons…First…"

If your theme is the need for renewed commitment to R&D, give three supporting projections to back up that theme—all based on the latest data and knowledge available right now.

Look into the Past

Looking into the past establishes credibility, and adds the gravitas of experience. People know early on that you have some depth, and recognize that you are probably worth listening to.

Example: "Fifteen years ago if I had tried to tell you that… A…you would have thought I was crazy. But 10 years ago we started to see…B…..And by 2005 the doors really started to open up with…C….and just two years ago…D….and today we are looking at a whole new world of opportunity that we never would have imagined back in _____. And by____ we could be seeing such vast changes that….E…."

In just a few seconds, this brief historical overview has made you an authority. You have stoked the audience's desire to hear more. Your message can't be far behind, and the floor is now yours.

Humor

Humor is risky in business, and as I said a minute ago, I would not recommend it. However, if you insist on trying to be funny, here are three basic rules to minimize your risk:

- ■ Always tell a joke as if it were true. That way, it can be a lot funnier when you get to the punch line, because your audience doesn't realize it's a joke.

- ■ Tell your funny story only to make a business point.

- ■ Never tell a joke at the expense of women or minorities (unless you are a woman or a minority member—and then only when you completely understand your audience).

The safest humor is self-effacing.

My advice would be that if you are in a business setting, skip the humor. Save it for weddings, toasts, roasts and private parties.

O One theme. Stick to just one message. Two or three is too many. But if you feel you have to talk about what you think are many themes, couch those "themes" in such a way that you sound like you are actually talking about your single theme in several different ways.

Example: "You can't talk about the need for a new commitment to R&D without also talking about….." (Insert your first sub theme here).

Then on to the next sub theme: "…The urgent need for renewed R&D I've been talking about is a factor in…" (Second sub theme here).

And so on. All the while, your message stays on track.

Never segue to a new category, and then another, with these familiar words we all know so well: "I would now like to turn to a different subject..." Why? Because you will abandon your theme and it will suddenly sound like you are really talking about four or five separate issues. If you want people to remember what you said, do not vary from your one theme.

I call this approach The Rocket. If you can picture a rocket, the nose cone carries the payload of the theme. Sub themes are housed under the nose cone and connected directly to it. The rocket looks something like this:

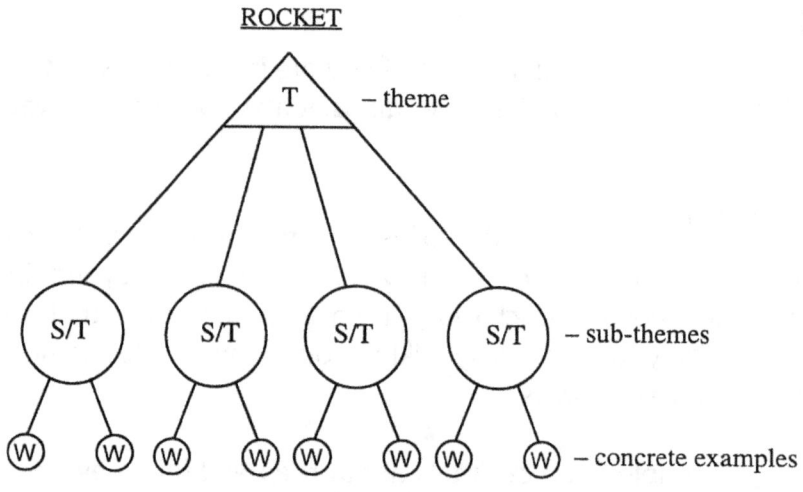

ROCKET

The Rocket makes many themes sound like one, which solves a lot of problems. But the simplest and most elegant approach is what I call The Necklace. The Necklace has no sub themes.

Imagine a silver cord. That's your theme. Next, string a bunch of pearls on that silver cord. Each pearl is an anecdote, illustration, or example that helps advance your theme. Like a good lawyer seeking to persuade a jury, you now pursue your message relentlessly with one pearl after another until you overwhelm all resistance. Then you can take your beginning and end and clasp them together for an intellectually complete design. The Necklace looks like this:

NECKLACE

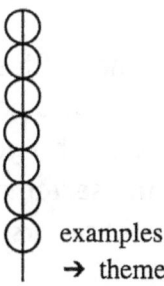

examples
→ theme

Historically, this very simple Necklace approach is the powerful psychological instrument leaders have unleashed to drive large numbers of people to victory on the battlefield, incite revolutions, triumph over tough odds, steer the policies of nations, and change the course of history. It can be equally effective in business.

W Windows. Windows are like the pearls in the Necklace. They let people get past ideas, concepts and generalities to bear witness to the concrete examples upon which you base your theme. Windows give you credibility, make you a lot more interesting, and ensure good retention.

So every time you offer up a concept, back it up. Deliver specific evidence you know your listeners will need to take action, make a choice, or say yes.

Concept: "…Our strategy is to increase profits, cut costs, and evaluate growth possibilities…"

Window: "…We've invested 28 million into our new innovation lab facility with 55 new products already under development…shed our non performing chemicals business at a savings this year alone of more than 200 million…automated our plants…and looked at several potential new partners…"

E Ear. The language of leaders has always been direct, unadorned, muscular and ordinary. You will rarely find a successful CEO, for example, who got to the top by talking like a memorandum, or in the secret language of his/her discipline. Great leaders are straight talkers. Ordinary language is straight talk. So talk straight.

In other words, be clear.

I sometimes ask people to relax and think of their "presentation" as if they were trying to sell their idea while having a beer in a bar with a buddy. Or in the hall at work, or at home in the kitchen over a cup of coffee.

You would be unlikely to say, for instance, "…In conclusion, dear, recent research indicates that it is incumbent upon us as a family to undertake measures that would have the effect of dampening unauthorized expenditures to reduce costs going forward…"

But you might say, "You know, I checked the bills and we've really got to try to keep a lid on costs for awhile…"

The only time language should obfuscate instead of clarify is when you need to dodge an issue, don't want to accept responsibility for something, or need to hide a problem.

Then, when all your options are exhausted, you can talk like a bureaucrat: "Relative to allegations regarding the implicit potential for resource allocation diminution and subsequent tangent departmental expenditure, it has been decided that while certain employees may have misspoken on this matter, further administrative departmental review and analysis is necessary on an ongoing basis relative to various established protocols before any performance evaluations or disciplinary action is undertaken..."

That may be a bit of exaggeration to make a point. But you get the idea. Translation: "...We caught people stealing from the company..."

While we're at it, let me add that you want to avoid "in conclusion" or "in summary" when you wrap things up. Instead, try, "...So it all comes down to this..." or, "...So here's my message...", or, "...Put it all together and here's what we've got..."

Why is this important? Because in normal conversation (see the kitchen example above) we don't say things like, "In conclusion" or, "In summary,"—unless you are the one in a thousand who actually talks that way in everyday speech.

R Retention. Your strong ending is as important as your strong beginning. This is what you want people to remember and walk away with. Can they pass a quiz on what you said three weeks from now? Do they know what you want them to do?

So don't get caught just winding down and stopping when you think you're done. That's an opportunity missed. You may get only one shot to sew up your covenant with your audience. You want people to say "wow" at the end, so always give them a good smack at the finish.

Here are six ways to end strongly:

1. **Sum up your message** ("So it all comes down to this...We still have time to close the R&D gap...It won't be easy, but if we act now we could be back on par with the rest of the industry in just three months, and leading the field again in just two years..."

2. **Loop back to your original device, such as a rhetorical question** ("So if I were to ask you again what keeps you up at night, I hope you can see now what I see...The real enemy isn't A or B or even C...The real enemy is D......and we have our last chance, right now, to do something about it and set things right...")

3. **Call for action** ("So I'm asking you to write the check to get R&D in this company back on its feet and leading the way as it did for 75 years...I'm asking you to put us on track to reclaim our legacy of creativity, innovation, and technical leadership...and I'm asking you to do it now so we can be up and running again by the fourth quarter..."

4. **Project into the future.** The cue for this one is different. The cue is, "So where do we go from here?.." Then you tell them where we go

("I see a very different company just two years from now...I see...A....B...and...C...But first we've all got to get behind the arrowhead to get this great institution back on the right track...").

5.   **Bad news/good news.** This will defuse potentially hostile questions by acknowledging any weaknesses that may be lurking in your "presentation." ("...So it all comes down to this... It is true that the new venture will have up front costs...and it's true that it may take months to assemble a team...and it's even true that we may already be too late....But most importantly it also true that this could be our last chance...If we are ever again to have a place at the table, this is our only hope...and we've got to act now.")

6.   **Tell a parable that rams home your message.** I'm not encouraging you to try this, because it is a little like humor, and could backfire if you don't tell the story with confidence and draw a clear link to your theme. But here's how it might work if, say, you were speaking to assembled employees and you needed to underscore the need for collaboration:

"What I'm saying reminds me of the story of the boy in ancient times who wanted to outwit the greatest wise man in the world, who lived in a cave on a mountain. The boy figured out a foolproof plan.

"He would take a pigeon to the wise man and ask if the pigeon were dead or alive. If the wise man said 'alive,' the boy would wring its neck. If the wise man said 'dead,' the boy would let it fly away.

"So the boy went to the entrance of the cave and shouted, 'O great master, I have a bird in my hands—Is it dead or alive?' And the response came back from the cave, 'Son, the answer is in your hands.'

(Pause)

"In a similar sense, the answer to where we go from here is now in your hands. I can not do this alone. I need your help. Together we have an opportunity to create something greater than we've ever made before. So let's get to work. Have at it—and I'll look forward to your preliminary reports on my desk by the end of the month."

Stories like this have impact. They can provide a powerful takeaway. But they can sound a little manipulative, even phony. And if you are not used to telling stories, you can see how a departure this might be hard to deliver seamlessly. So resist the temptation to dive in with a parable until you feel comfortable, and have the right parable and the confidence to pull it off.

I have designed the entire POWER Formula (all the above) to automatically put you on a conversational footing with your audience. This is exactly where you want to be. If so far we have managed to disguise our "presentation" as a conversation, then we are already way ahead of the game.

That's the architecture, which tells us what our basic "presentation" should look like. But what if we want to use visual aids? Then we have to adapt the principles of what I call the Foundation. Here's what that looks like.

The Foundation

The foundation is easy to remember and based on just three simple rules:

■ **Rule One:** Begin and end your talk with no graphs or slides on the wall or screen, and no open presentation books on the table.

■ **Rule two:** Get rid of all word slides (but keep them in the document). Use only graphics, schematics, photos, etc. on the wall or in the presentation book.

■ **Rule three:** Introduce the NEXT slide while the CURRENT SLIDE is still on the wall—or while the current page is still open in the presentation book.

So let's say you find yourself on a stage in front of an audience. The slide on the wall behind you should show only your "cover page"—perhaps your company logo, with your name and title. This forces the audience to pay attention to you (because you have given them no option). With no distractions behind you, you have the floor. You are free to begin strongly and command the room with the stage to yourself. After your strong start (see P in POWER, page two), which may consist of a personal story, an anecdote and a strong statement to define your theme, and last a couple of minutes, you will say something like, "...as you can see here," or "...take a look at this...." Then you click to your first graphic slide (or turn to your first graphic page if you happen to be sitting in a conference or meeting room).

Your graphics should support your theme and make a convincing case with the audience. Select only those pictures that help prove your case. Trend lines showing changes and projections, for example. All non-essential slides are consigned to the document (more on that in a moment), which you can hand out later. Soon you will have worked your way down through your pictures.

Along the way, you will give a brief intro to the each next (new) slide while the current (old) slide is still up. For example, you might say (sales slide is up):"...So while sales in the third quarter were up more than six percent over the same time last year, market share was actually down about two percent..." CLICK. Now you pause for a moment. The sales slide is gone. The marketing slide is up. The audience digests what you just said, while adjusting to the marketing slide.

Then you may throw in a line like, "...You can see that we actually began to lose market share as early as January..."

As you progress through the slide show, your listeners are also getting the distinct impression that you are in control of the show, and that the show is not in control of you. This is good.

At some point you will say something like, "...So it all comes down to this..." Now you click again and up pops your "cover page"—the same one you started with.

Or you could go to a blue or black slide. The point is that you will not end with a graphic or word slide. You will end with just you talking. No graphs. No word slides. Just you wrapping up with a strong ending.

I call this the Oreo (we will talk a little more about the Oreo shortly). You are the chocolate, top and bottom. Your pictures are the cream filling in the middle.

The Foundation and the Oreo will do the job for you. They are your ground rules. But don't stop there. Never feel obliged to hold back your own creative ideas. For example, depending on the situation and the audience, you could pick a video with voice and music to open your "presentation," and pepper it with little DVD clips, animation or photo images throughout. You could even have another video with sound at the end—as long as everything you throw in only adds to the critical mission of driving home your message. A caution about digital animation: using clever animation strictly to amuse or entertain could actually have the effect of detracting from your purpose and message.

Now you know what it takes to create the Perfect Presentation. You are already 75 percent to your goal. The rest is execution. So let's look at how to apply some of these ideas in everyday business practice.

Chapter 2
Selling Product or Service

The problem with most "presentations" is that people talk too much about themselves or their companies and too little about what they can do for the people listening. Truth be told, most of us have made this mistake at some point in our careers.

We have often overlooked a core truth—it is NOT about us. It's about them. If we survive long enough, we all eventually come to the realization that if we serve the client, we serve ourselves.

This is easy to forget, for example, if you wind up in a bake-off and it's down to you and one or two competitors. Self-interest kicks in at the expense of service to the client. The client typically doesn't care how great we think we are, or how cool our technology is, or how neat our product is. He only cares about what we can do for him.

Most often, he only cares about whether we can help him make money or save money, or both.

So the great "presentation" will always be about the client.

That's point one. Point two is that if you threw away your presentation books and never used them again you would probably do yourself a favor (that's why God created golf—more business gets done on golf courses than in all the board rooms in the world).

But let's assume that for different reasons you can't toss your presentation books. It could happen, for example, that the client demands books in advance of meetings, or that junior people may need the books in order to adhere to the party line. Or you may simply want to provide a book for people to write notes on and take home for reference.

People on the receiving end of typical financial pitches (hedge funds or private equity firms trying to raise capital, for example) will often tell you they gag silently when confronted with "presentations" as fat as phone books. This initial shock sets up an aura of frustration from the beginning, which could sabotage any hope of success—even if you think you and your team were brilliant.

So what to do?

First, understand—particularly in financial services presentations—that you are going to need a much slimmer book. In the end, you will actually have two books—a Waffle and a Wafer.

The Wafer is in effect the official record. Let's call it the document. The Wafer is what you use to give your presentation.

Here's how you create the Wafer:

- Dump all the word slides (50 0r 60 pages could disappear right there—and don't worry, those word slides never go away. I'll explain shortly).

- Use only graphics, schematics, charts, photos, anything visual.

- Make sure that all the pictures you choose advance the theme of your conversation. If, for example, your theme is personalized service on a global scale, every slide you show should help drive home that point. The theme should cascade from picture to picture. In this way, you are like a good lawyer presenting evidence, one piece of proof at a time.

- Blow up all your charts etc. so that they practically fill the entire page. Get rid of the words and bullets on all picture slides (but they stay in the Waffle, which will be your official document).

- Eliminate agendas in slides and in books (keep them in the much bigger document).

- Move your strongest slides—those which best complement your theme—to the top.

Now you've got a thin "presentation" book and a fat document. The thin document is for use in the real-time "presentation". After changes, it could end up being just 8 or 10 pages long. The official (original) document, however—the Waffle—will remain perhaps 100 pages long. The Waffle can be useful in Q and A and as a reference source.

If for any reason you feel you must use the Waffle in the "presentation", you can soften the blow by referring to only a handful of specific pages (any misguided effort to work your way through an entire Waffle will certainly be met with quiet rage and certain failure. In fact, tolerance for long, windy presentations has never been lower than it is today, and it should not come as a surprise if the offender were suddenly interrupted and told to get to the point and wrap things up). The only exceptions might be an exhaustive Six Sigma quality control presentation, or an all-day engineering or technical report, or analysis.

You could leave the Waffle with clients as a physical or digital takeaway. You may also choose to leave the Wafer, as well.

...

Now that you've got your "presentation" book straightened out, it's time to make your case. Here's the approach I would recommend:

If you are "presenting" in a conference room or similar facility, get introductions out of the way if possible before you even sit down. The reason for this is that introductions after you are seated add an undesirable air of formality to the proceedings, and detract from your opportunity to get off to a strong start. So while you are saying hi and shaking hands, introduce one another and get some of the chit-chat and amenities out of the way before you take your places at the table.

Once seated, if the client wishes to engage in further social talk, about the weather, or whatever, that's fine. Oblige him. Let him set the tone. But at the first sign that the time has come to get on with it, be prepared to launch.

At this point, you have options. You could begin strongly using any combination of ideas from the POWER Formula (see page 3), which will always serve you well. Or you could take a different tack and start by asking a question, such as, "How do you think we might be most helpful to you...?" This second option sometimes strikes an appealing emotional chord, warms the room immediately to your favor, and focuses the spotlight on the client, where it belongs.

Once you have the floor, by all means do NOT waste everyone's time with predictable and useless drivel, such as, "Good morning. It is a pleasure to be here. We want to thank you for this opportunity to make this presentation..." NO!

Why not? Because you rob yourself of your moment of greatest impact. Because almost everybody else does it. And because NOBODY WANTS TO HEAR A PRESENTATION (which is—as I have pointed out earlier—often viewed with not a little disappointment, even contempt, as just a boilerplate created by somebody else). Rather than seizing the opportunity to get closer to your client, you have only managed to set up an invisible psychological barrier that will likely get the whole thing off to a numbing and disheartening start (of course no one will actually tell you that).

If you do elect to ask the opening pertinent question and turn the "presentation" into an interactive conversation right off the bat, you must now be prepared not only to listen, but to skillfully move forward. Follow your theme faithfully to reveal all the ways that your firm's talents, experience and brainpower can help the client. Fielding questions in this ongoing dialogue, while constantly ushering the conversation ahead to meet the constant press of time requirements will require a deft touch. So this approach is often most effective in the hands of experienced senior people.

That's just one more reason why the more junior the presenter, the more the need for the "presentation" book. As far as the client is concerned, the person you send from your company IS your company. So it would be unwise ever to entrust an important sale to a newbie, who may not only be unprepared to represent your firm properly, or incapable of fielding questions effectively, but may also send the wrong signal to a potential new client that the relationship is not being taken seriously.

As a rule, the more senior the "presenter", the higher the likelihood for a successful outcome, and the lower the risk that something might go terribly wrong. Grievous setbacks caused by inexperienced, unprepared or unqualified players occur with distressing regularity, and certainly more often than most businesses would be prepared to admit.

Importantly, I have often found that senior people can be far more effective with no props whatsoever. In fact, they can actually debilitate themselves the minute they open a presentation book.

Psychologically, clients want to believe that any senior person sitting (or standing) in front of them has the depth, background and expertise to make any "presentation" book not only redundant but irrelevant. In the worst case scenarios, very good, but misguided, "presenters" unwittingly bury themselves—and their prospects—under a toxic garbage heap of endless word slides.

Some of the most successful financial services pitches, to raise money or get new business, for example, (we're not talking about CFO presentations to the board or investors in this case) are made by senior people, and take no more than 10 or 15 minutes. Often a book is nowhere to be seen.

So you can see that your presentation book—or visual aids of any kind, for that matter—can sometimes be more of a liability than an asset, as we will see shortly.

You may even have the misfortune to discover that the "presentation" book accomplishes the exact opposite of your objectives. In other words, depending on circumstances, you may sometimes find that it works against you, rather than for you.

But what if the client demands copies of the book in advance or requests that it be placed on the table before the meeting starts?

In that case, here is what you do. Let's assume that you've got the signal to start.

If the books are on the table, you may notice that some people in the room are already leafing through the pages. You must put a stop to that. I suggest you say something like, "Before we get into the books, there are a few things I would like to say first…"

Or: "If you could put the books aside for a moment, I'd like to take a moment to give you the big picture…"

This is your opportunity to run all the way down the field with the ball. You've got everyone's attention and you should use it to your advantage. This means taking the next minute or two to TELL THE WHOLE STORY—BEFORE YOU EVER INVITE YOUR AUDIENCE TO OPEN THE BOOK.

This is a neat trick practiced by some of the best leadership communications pros in business. The best "presenters" never fail to give a short version of their pitch at the very top— IN CASE THEY ARE INTERUPTED OR RUN OUT OF TIME.

Your listeners don't know it, but they have heard everything they have to hear to make a decision or take action— before they ever even see the first page. Not only does this approach have a powerful effect on the listener, but it is your insurance that your time and efforts will not have been in vain should the unexpected suddenly pop up (which, when you think about it, we can almost expect—especially in business).

So a good start would incorporate the leverage of the P in the POWER Formula (strong start) and, for good measure, leave no doubt about the theme (the O). From the time you start until your first graphic (assuming you choose to use visual aids of any kind), you will have satisfied the answers these questions: Why should they listen? What is my message? What is the takeaway? What, if anything, do I want them to do?

Then you are saying something like, "…Let me show you what I mean…" and you are into the Wafer (or naming a particular page number, if you find you can not escape having to use the Waffle document).

Now you are sprinting straight to the goal. Your job here is simply to use each page of the book to pursue your case and support your message. I'm not talking about simply delivering information. I'm talking about folding all that relevant information into a theme and throwing in data, illustrations, analogies, examples and stories to make your points, all of which must be tied directly to your theme.

When you are done with the book, simply close it, pause, catch your breath, look around the room and say something like, "…So it all comes down to this…"; or, "…So here's the message…"' or, "…Put it all together and here's what we've got…"

Your ending should be strong. It should be not only what it all comes down to, but maybe also what you want the people to take away. This is the R in the POWER Formula.

Sometimes I suggest that in smaller or more intimate settings—in a conference room, for example—that after you have told your audience what it all comes down to, or asked them to pursue a particular action, you might finally wrap it up with a very simple little question: "…So what do you think?" In a selling situation this could trigger a productive conversation. At the very least, your listeners might simply respond that will have to think it over and get back to you. Either way, you have nothing to lose.

In a perfect world—if you stick to the POWER Formula— you may never have to use the book or show a single slide on the screen. But chances are, you will choose to use at least a few slides, or refer to some supporting graphs in the book. In that case, be sure to apply the Foundation. You start without slides. You end without slides. Banish word slides to the official document. If you use slides, put them in the middle. This is the Oreo we were talking about.

But what if you are not alone?

If you've come as a member of a team, it is important that you give the perception that you really are a team.

This means not only investing a little time to plan and rehearse, but also to perform SEAMLESSLY. What I mean is, instead of saying, "…now I'd like to turn the presentation over to Ellen, who will talk about…" Ellen just picks up on the conversation right where you left off. Ellen says, "…at the same time we are seeing…" and now all eyes and ears are on Ellen. It's almost as if you are reading each others' thoughts and speaking in one voice. Then somebody else jumps in as if on cue (and it is on cue). People watching are thinking, this is different, these guys are good.

Now they are thinking the magic words: I like these guys. Possibly the most important words in business. This is the prize you have been seeking, and it is worth talking about for a moment.

Once you achieve "good guy" status (gender is irrelevant) you become part of a special club—and your prospects improve measurably. Once inside the "good guy" club the old rules are out and all kinds of lucrative possibilities are suddenly on the table. You have stepped into the world of what I call business likeability. Likeability is far more powerful factor in business relationships than intellectual acumen. And it comes through conversations, not "presentations".

It is virtually IMPOSSIBLE to achieve likeability by giving a (conventional) " presentation." Golf may do it. A nice meal may do it. A walk around the block might do it. Even a beer in a bar or a chance meeting on a plane may do it. But a presentation certainly will not.

The ONLY way for a "presentation" to do it, is to make it feel and sound like ordinary language (conversational approach). Most people will not buy your service or product until they first buy you. In my experience, the record consistently affirms that the person armed with this knowledge has a deal-making and game-breaking edge every time.

Now you should be able to top the performance of any competitor, selling any service or product to any audience.

Chapter 3
Reporting Up Within The Organization

This is the arena where thousands of careers are made—or inadvertently damaged—every year.

Most people underestimate the value of the internal "presentation" to influence promotion, status and compensation. Most people incorrectly conclude that when they have finished rattling off the information requested, they have also discharged their duty.

They have not. In fact, they have failed to recognize an opportunity.

At best, they have probably only succeeded in making themselves even more faceless, and more forgettable, in a crowd of peers. At worst, they have marked themselves for eventual extermination.

At their peril, tens of thousands of otherwise well-meaning managers around the world continue to ignore what should be the obvious: that it is never enough simply to deliver information.

We've all suffered through the bloated groaners that seem to take forever, tell us nothing, are near impossible to fathom, and go nowhere. We don't know what we are supposed to do, nor think. The next day, we can't even pass a quiz on what happened. In fact, the "presenter" could have stayed home and sent a memo or email instead, for all the good it did.

Certainly not a good investment of our precious time and productivity.

Yet for all our frustration and annoyance, the poor guy who inflicts this misery upon us probably has no idea that he has ventured into treacherous territory. That's because he is only doing what everyone has always done, in the exact way it has always been done, going back who knows how many years. Whether he is reporting on the last quarter or giving a market overview, he winds up stuck in a rut he doesn't even know he's in. Nor does he have the wherewithal to escape— even if he did know.

Paradoxically, if he follows the traditional approach—that is, if he adheres to the conventions and expectations of his own corporate culture, he is likely to fall short of his potential—in spite of all his brains and talent.

Demonstrably smart, for example, but perhaps unable to lead or inspire. Perhaps full of good ideas but unable to effectively sell those ideas to decision makers.

Any reasonable person might ask, how can that possibly be that brains and talent might not prevail?

The answer is that the typical internal down-up presentation is one of the biggest missed career opportunities in business today.

Here's why: Let's say you are on the agenda for the next management meeting to report on departmental results for the third quarter. You know how this goes. It goes the same way it has always gone. When your turn comes you give a lot of facts and review a lot of numbers—so many facts and numbers, in fact, that you create a huge jellyfish of random information.

It takes a while to get through all this stuff, but that's okay, because that's all anyone expects. You begin at the beginning, then grind your way methodically and chronologically down through all three months, careful to connect all the dots, until you finally wind up at the end. Then you answer a few questions and sit down.

It seems like a sensible approach.

So if it ain't broke, why fix it?

Because it is broke.

Even a casual observer of this egregious waste of management time might note that after two hours, nothing of recognizable value had occurred.

In fact, an observant eight year old could tell you that when you boil it all down, all the guy said was that nothing of particular interest had changed since the last quarter, with the exception of a competitor's product and distribution challenge in the Southeast. This eight year old might translate the entire pro-forma "presentation" into a simple couple of sentences: "Nothing has really changed. But Vista has made a push into the southeast, so we're beefing up marketing in the Atlanta office."

So how do we fix this mess and morph a jellyfish into an arrowhead?

First, the smart player ADDS VALUE BY DELIVERING A MESSAGE BASED ON WHAT ALL THAT INFORMATION MEANS. This means that you owe it to yourself and your listeners to TRANSLATE all that goop into one simple idea. It's up to you to glean the bottom line, attach a business message to it, then make sure your audience gets it and understands it.

It's unproductive just to throw INFORMATION at people. They don't want it and can't handle it. Business leaders do not want subordinates to drop a ton of data on their heads, and then leave them to try to figure out themselves. Actually, they want YOU to figure it out. They may not come right out and tell you, but what they want is your brains, so that all that information can now become profitable business KNOWLEDGE.

Knowledge is the secret treasure locked inside every bad presentation. Mostly likely, your management has been a little busy with other things lately. So when you're doing the talking, they look to you for more than the wheelbarrow you just emptied on the table. They would appreciate a little help trying to make productive business sense of all the possible opportunities, answers and solutions locked inside that shapeless mass.

To understand the important difference between information and knowledge, imagine a huge jar full of thousands of pieces of confetti. In that jar, mixed with the confetti, are a dozen tiny, shiny metallic chips. Put a magnet to the side of the jar and all the shiny chips suddenly leap against the glass. If you think of the confetti as information, the chips are knowledge. And you are the magnet. You have extracted knowledge from information.

Team leaders, division heads, senior officers all want chips, not confetti. They want someone who can make sense of all that data, come to conclusions, and have someone—YOU—articulate those conclusions so they can make better decisions.

So look at the information. Think about what you see. Do you spot any trends? Do you see changes, new situations, opportunities, danger signs, bright spots, anomalies, notable consistencies, inconsistencies, likely projections, anything that can help your management make intelligent choices that will lead the company in a winning direction? What does all this information mean? What's it all about? What kind of a story is this big beluga of data trying to tell me?

We call the consistent ability to derive knowledge from information WISDOM. Smart business leaders love wisdom, and they will kill to get it and to keep it.

So listen to what the numbers are telling you and know your story.

The story could be that sales are up over the last quarter, but market share is down. Or that a segment of the market is starting to eclipse other segments. Or that nothing at all is happening, everything is flat—and that is a story in itself. Maybe the fact that we are not going anywhere tells us that we are misreading the market or missing opportunities in sales and marketing, or new product development.

Your story becomes your conversation.

When you tell your story, you will want to underscore your observations, make pertinent suggestions, give counsel, make projections—all based on your analysis—to help steer the decision-making process to where you think it needs to go.

If you do this, you can distinguish yourself in important ways.

Where yesterday you may have been no more than an anonymous middle manager viewed as a mere functionary by your senior management, today you are seen in a completely different light. Today you are suddenly visible. And because of your initiative and helpful guidance—your ability, say, to spot an opportunity emerging out of a developing trend—you have established yourself as a valued member of the leadership team, even though you may not actually have the rank nor seniority.

When you spare your management having to ask you what it all means, and what we perhaps ought to be doing about it, you have bestowed the gift of time saved, for which they will be forever grateful. In business, time above all things is the commodity most prized, because it really is money.

Increased compensation and promotion frequently follow as a natural next step.

Everybody can add value and boost their careers exponentially this way, but not everyone wants to. Some people don't want to stand out, take risks or become any more visible than they have to. They would prefer to remain anonymous, well out of the limelight, collect a bi-weekly paycheck and dodge responsibility all the way to retirement (if they make it that far).

These people may tell you that the way you are proposing to pitch to management is not the way it has always been done, or that the corporate culture would frown on something new and different, might even be hostile. Or that it won't work because management is expecting something entirely different. They might be right on all counts. But my advice to you is to pay no attention.

You will find these people are the majority in every company you will ever work. They are the indispensable worker bees among us, and we should all value their contributions, because free enterprise and nature itself require more worker bees than leaders. Every company on earth would collapse without them.

But worker bees are precisely the same people who will never see that their objections are all the more reason for people like you to seize the career chance, break with tradition, and rise up and shine—whether you are a team leader reporting to a department head, or senior vice president of a large-cap company "presenting" to your chairman and board.

Worker bees are content with things as they are. But for those who live to test themselves, get excited about new possibilities, love daily challenges, think a little competition is a good thing, believe in meritocracy and tend to lean towards the optimistic, they will profit by daring to be different.

Who will complain if your "presentation" is brief, interesting and useful—instead of long, boring and useless?

The bottom line is that those oft-dreaded moments of reporting up within your organization that everyone seems to loathe are among are the best chances you will ever have to capitalize on your stealth skills, be seen and heard in the best possible light, and actually make a difference. They should never be underestimated.

This should be reason enough for anyone to rethink how they put together and deliver internal "presentations". But I see an even more compelling argument. The smart conference room player reporting up to senior management violates traditional rules in another important way—by FLIPPING THE WHOLE THING AROUND. Turning it right on its head.

Instead of talking about what's already happened (but wait—wasn't that the assignment?) he launches in a different direction—and gets everybody's attention—by PROJECTING INTO THE FUTURE.

But why? Why would anybody want to just jump right into the future when your listeners haven't even had a chance to hear about the past?

There are a number of answers:

—- A benchmark of real leadership is a consistent eye to the future (a business asset like no other). This road ahead is the domain of the thinker and strategist, and senior managers love futurists. By positioning yourself as someone who looks first to the future, you have drawn attention to yourself as a potential future leader.

—- The leaders in your business probably already have a pretty good idea in advance of what you are going to say. So they don't need a tutorial. A rehash—especially a droning, rambling, unfocussed rehash, or an exhaustive detailing of the numbers category by category, no matter how irrelevant—is unproductive (with the singular exception of all-day budget drill-downs, or 6-Sigma forensic analysis meetings). What they really want to know is, What's new? Where are we headed? And what should we do?

When you begin with the future, you have the advantage of getting directly to solutions. This is where the rubber hits the road. Going straight to solutions tends to shorten the process. You will always win allies by beefing up the business value of your message, while slashing the length of time it takes to tell it.

Of course, it goes without saying that any projections you venture must be reasonable, doable, defensible, without exaggeration, and based on solid fact.

Naturally, your senior team will be expecting to hear the same old same old. They will brace themselves for the predictable flurry of data representing the summary of last quarter, delivered in numbing detail and left to the decision-makers to decipher.

But the talented "presenter" confounds all expectations by jumping at this opportunity to PAINT INSTEAD A PICTURE OF WHAT'S COMING—BASED ON WHAT HAS ALREADY HAPPENED (THE INFORMATION HIS AUDIENCE WAS EXPECTING TO HEAR FIRST).

He will then draw conclusions and suggest courses of action.

So instead of something predictable like, "Today I am going to present the results of the 3rd Quarter..." followed by a routine chronological regurgitation of data, I would suggest a vastly more useful and more productive approach that goes something like this:

"In the next eighteen months we're looking at a window of opportunity to gain market share in the Southeast, cut costs at our plants in Ohio and Indiana, and widen our distribution on the West Coast...We are seeing competitive store advantages emerging that weren't there just a few months ago, favorable labor and technology developments in manufacturing, and positive legislative news in California and Oregon...

"...I'm basing these conclusions on what has been happening in the last three months...Let me show you what I mean...."

Now you cite specific indicators from the data to support your case. If you make a good enough case, you may not have to follow the usual rules, which would mean descending into a tedious pro forma review of every last piece of information in the presentation. But if you are required to cover all the bases formally, at least you got off to a brilliant start.

As you can see in this example, once you know your story, you might be amazed to find how little time you need to tell it.

Again, your management is now looking at you in a very different way.

Because this approach is different, you can expect flak.

One of the first objections you are likely to hear is that if you don't use a lot of time (or use all your allotted time), somehow you may come across as superficial or unprepared. These people will argue that management will expect, even demand a line-by-line formal review (and because of any number of embedded cultural biases, they may be correct).

I have seen hundreds of examples in which individual clients dared—admittedly with some trepidation—to go the short route, only to be rewarded handsomely. In just one example, I managed to persuade a department head in a Fortune 10 company to slash his regular Tuesday morning report from 45 minutes to less than 10. He fully expected to be greeted with a verbal spanking, or worse, for this startling and unexpected departure from the norm. Instead, he got a round of thanks and words of appreciation from all 26 senior people in the room, beginning with the chairman, and a promotion a month later to vice president. Today, four years later, he is chairman himself, and CEO. And he's still a client.

The message here is that short is almost always better than long. On top of that, if you shorten your "presentation", you now not only have plenty of time for Q & A to fall back on (Q & A is where most people feel they perform best), but you've also got the added insurance of the original hard copy document, which you can refer to at any time and whenever necessary.

So you are covered.

Keep in mind also that front-loading your report with your conclusions and recommendations—rather than forcing your audience to wait until the end to get to the only part they really care about (message and solutions)—protects you from the unkindest cut of all: being suddenly interrupted by an impatient vice president demanding that you get to the point. You are also insured against disaster in the event you run out of time.

The fact is that you can always be brief—and far more effective—without sacrificing substance or credibility.

Chapter 4

Use Visual Aids so They Work for, and Never Against You.

The whole idea behind visual aids is that they should aid, not hinder. But too often they can be more of a problem than a solution.

That's why I recommend that you use PowerPoint, slides, presentation books, handouts or samples only when you feel you must. There can be no doubt that visual aids, when used correctly, can pump life and color into any presentation. But as you may have noticed, most often they are NOT used correctly (you know you're doing something wrong if your audience becomes bored, restless or impatient. This is especially true in the case of PowerPoint).

As I said, for visual aids to be more of an asset than a liability, you may have to change old habits and thinking.

The biggest problems emerge out of PowerPoint, so let's look at PowerPoint first.

PowerPoint as a tool was, and is, a good idea. Executed properly, it can add value. But in the hands of most business people, it's a good idea gone bad. That's because very few people understand how to unleash the power in PowerPoint. So your average PowerPoint presentation, paradoxically, can wind up doing more harm than good. For example, a very smart team with a great product or service could blow one opportunity after another and not realize until too late—if ever—what the real problem is. In fact, there may be plenty of problems, which on the surface may seem benign, but could be deadly. Here are some of them:

- Word slides are a killer and should be avoided at all costs. You will hear the argument that word slides, because they are visual, double your effectiveness and create reinforcement. Not so. In fact, word slides actually slash your effectiveness and create REDUNDENCY.

- Words slides distract from the speaker. Given a chance, people will read whatever you put on the wall, because the eye is more powerful than the ear. When you audience is reading, you can't compete with your own show—because most people are incapable of reading and trying to listen to you at the same time. So you demean your value by simply becoming a droning sound. You might as well have sent them a memo. Worse, most people will have read the entire page while you are still on the first or second sentence or bullet. So you are also out of sync with your audience.

- As if that weren't enough, if you use word slides you give the impression that you are simply reading or paraphrasing what someone else has written for you. In other words, you rob yourself of an opportunity to be seen as an authority or leader— particularly if you are a senior person—and send the message that you can't talk about your own area of expertise without scripted props and a crutch.

■ And the further up you go, the more egregious the offence. No CEO should ever be caught dead using words slides. Even vice presidents and department heads could do without when talking to employees and customers—but probably not when speaking to boards, senior management, investors or analysts. In these cases, relevant graphics would be helpful to reveal supporting financial data, for example.

As I said earlier, you should toss them out of your actual presentation, but keep them in the document, which you can refer to in Q and A (question and answer) and hand out afterwards.

EXCEPTIONS TO THE WORD SLIDE RULE:

A. When you don't have photos, and want to show a list of the names of participants (a team that performed particularly well, for instance).

B. When you are in a big room and people 100 feet away may be having trouble trying to keep up with what's happening on the stage. In that case you might want to put up huge banner slides that read NEXT STEPS or CHALLENGES or OPPORTUNITIES while you expound on these issues.

C. When you want to show newspaper or magazine headlines.

D. When you want to quote someone, and feel the quote is so important you would rather show it for emphasis rather than say it. In that case, you might say, for example, "...And I think the Fed chairman nailed it right on the head with this quote last week, which is sure to be the center of debate for months to come..." Then you CLICK the slide and stop talking. Let them read and absorb the quote in silence for a few seconds—to embed and underscore the idea behind the quote (which, of course, is directly related to your message).

- Stick to one graphic on the screen at a time—unless you want to show contrast (a large pie chart next to a smaller pie chart to highlight growth, for example) and you can be sure everybody can see important details on the screen from the back of the room. At the very least, design your slides so they can be read at a glance from 35 feet away.

- Don't be persuaded that trying to shove four slides on one slide is a good idea because it shortens the number of slides. It may indeed reduce the number of slides, but it will also miniaturize your data so that from the audience's perspective it is also, as a practical matter, almost useless. At the same time, you might be able to get away with four slides on the page in a presentation book (because the audience is physically very close to the page).

- Use highly complex or cluttered slides only when you are trying to emphasis a valid business point—for example, when a process is so Byzantine it has ceased to be productive. You may also choose to highlight a cluttered slide to reveal the enormous amount of exhaustive research or analysis that went into the development of a particular product or service. But do not dwell on the slide. Show it only to make a quick impression.

■   Slides can be useful, but not so helpful when they contradict or diminish what you are trying to do. What you should be trying to do is clarify and support your message. So make sure your slides do not obfuscate, nor muddy your message. If the slides you chose do not qualify as proof or evidence to support your proposition, then they are merely supplemental background information, and belong in the document—not on the screen or in the book.

■   Don't try to mix and match words and pictures. For example, don't show a pie chart with a lot of bullets or text. You can certainly mix and match all you like in your document, but never in your actual "presentation". If you must mix and match, then it is better to do so in the presentation book—because, again, your audience will only be a foot or so away from the page.

■   Make sure you capitalize on the psychological power of size to underscore your evidence. Fill as much space on the screen or on the page as possible.

■   Avoid precious pastel colors such as puce, mauve, lilac, lime, violet, rose, lavender or pink (unless you have good business reason to do so—if, for example, you are in the cosmetics industry. But even then, if you are presenting to your board, you would want to favor primary colors). The most substantial-looking and elegant tones are black, royal blue, dark blue, yellow, red, green, gold, orange and white.

- Dark blue or black backgrounds are not only more upscale, but they also avoid the garish glare that can come with white screens, especially in darkened rooms. A harsh (and unflattering) white light can easily overwhelm the speaker, attracting too much attention where it often does not belong. You do not want to be seen as subordinate to your show, particularly in the wrong light.

- Keep charts and schematics simple. For example, you can always eliminate the north and east line borders on charts and mark time, dollar or quantity sequences every 10, 50 or 100, instead of each individual measurement or calibration.

- Slides that try to show two or more different measurements on the same chart (the left border representing cost containment, for instance, while the right reveals something else) are usually counterproductive and should be avoided. But it's ok if your management is accustomed to this approach, or for the document. In fact, you can put almost anything you like and as much as you like in the document.

- If you are disciplined and judicious, you should rarely need more than five to eight slides in any presentation. At the same time, your Waffle can have 100 slides.

- Put ALL your slides in the MIDDLE of your show (the Oreo cookie we talked about earlier). This allows you to get off to a strong start and wrap things up with a powerful ending. That said, there may be occasions when you might want to put a powerful message-related visual or video on the wall even before you begin speaking. Barring that, you should begin and end with a simple logo slide or even just a blank black or dark blue side.

■ Highlight important numbers by using a different color (as a rule, green represents good financial news. Red means not so good). For added emphasis, make select numbers or words bigger.

■ Be mindful of the fact that your audience needs you to be a good guide to help them navigate and know what they are supposed to be looking at any given time. For instance, you might say, "… As you can see down here in the right hand corner…" or, "…Take a look at the big green slice of the pie…" or, "…This picture is a little busy, but the only numbers that matter to us are in yellow at the bottom of the second column…"

■ Make sure your trend lines and graph lines of any kind are thick enough to they don't look wispy and insubstantial. All lines should be unambiguous and easy to see. Colors are almost always better than simple black and white.

■ Cartoons just for the sake of humor can be a liability—unless you can make the case that they unquestionably support the theme. Then go ahead and have some fun.

■ Avoid anything that resembles a computer game—unless you are in the computer game business. Animation should always be kept on a tight leash if it distracts from the message or threatens to overwhelm the presentation and the presenter.

■ For general audiences—arguably less so for heavily quant-weighted financial or management audiences—- arrows are a good choice to show things going up or down in a big way.

- As a rule, the better the execution of the Power Formula, the less the need for visual aids of any kind, including PowerPoint.

Chapter 5
Prepared Text

Avoid it if you can.

Of course, there will be occasions when you may not have a choice. You may have little or no time to prepare. Or strict time constraints. Or you may not want to run the risk of saying something you didn't want to say, or omitting something you did want to say. You may have to testify on a delicate issue, or deliver a scientific paper, or follow a party line that has been dictated by lawyers (who are particularly sensitive to choice of words). Or you may be too petrified to do it any other way. Whatever the reason, if you are a business person, you will likely find yourself in a situation some day where you can not escape having to use a written speech.

But even if you do it well, you are still trapped behind a lectern and you will still probably look like you are reading (in more formal circumstances, you may not have a choice). A slave to your text, you are denied the opportunity to walk out and command the whole stage, and you wind up physically shut off from your audience. This only heightens the perception that you are engaged in a PRESENTATION and not a CONVERSATION. This puts up a negative psychological barrier and diminishes your presence in the room.

Yet there are benefits. If you learn the technique, you need very little preparation time. Plus, you will be certain to stay within your time limit, and you will say exactly what you want to say. So even if you end up stuck to your text, you can still pull it off with grace and style.

The trick is simply to deliver your prepared text so you will NOT look like you are reading, which should amp your eye contact exponentially, and magically morph the whole exercise into what appears to be a conversation—even though you are reading every word on the page. This virtue in itself can win you considerable purchase with any audience. The concept is easy, but you may have to practice to get it right.

First, prepare your speech so you can read it from three or four feet away. This means blowing the words up to 26 font size, double-spacing between lines, triple-spacing between paragraphs, making each sentence a separate paragraph, never letting a sentence run on to the next page, and putting page numbers in all four corners. You may only get three sentences on a page, and you will use more paper. But it will be worth it, because these changes will make any text VERY EASY to read. They will also help make the little trick I'm about to show you easy to execute.

Your text should look something like this:

This is an example of the prepared text type face and format.

You will note that sentences are separate—double spaced between lines, triple spaced between para-graphs.

Sentences end on the page—they do not track over to the next page.

Page numbers are in all four corners.

Now take your speech, wrap it around the thigh AWAY from your audience so that it is at least partially hidden and step up to the podium.

Don't look down. Look out at the people. Smile if it comes naturally (if it doesn't, you will look tense trying to force a smile, so skip the smile). Ease the speech up to the lectern. Move slowly. Try not to let your audience see what you are doing. Take in plenty of oxygen through your nose. Relax.

If you are right-handed, stack the speech to the left of the lectern as you continue to look around the room. Then with the fingers of your right hand take your top page and place it to the right. From now on, you will be sliding pages left to right using your right hand (or right to left, using your left hand, if you are left-handed).

This operation has created a pause, which piques audience interest.

You have already memorized your first couple of sentences, so there is no need to look down as you begin to speak. If you do look down, you drastically soften your moment of greatest impact.

Now the magic begins. Because from now on, instead of doing what everyone else does—- look down at a sentence, start talking, then come up for air, and then go back down again to finish the sentence—YOU ARE GOING TO REVERSE THE PROCESS.

BY CONTRAST, YOU ARE GOING TO GLANCE DOWN, COMMIT THE FIRST THIRD OR HALF OF THE SENTENCE TO SHORT TERM MEMORY, LOOK UP, SPEAK THE WORDS, THEN LET YOUR

EYES GO BACK DOWN TO READ WORDS IN THE MIDDLE OF THE SENTENCE, THEN COME BACK UP WITH YOUR EYES TO FINISH THE END OF THE SENTENCE. YOU ARE GOING TO DO THIS IN ONE SEAMLESS, UNHURRIED SWEEP THAT MIMICS THE WAY YOU NORMALLY TALK (keep the brakes on, because we typically read a lot faster than we talk).

If the sentence is short (see sample above) then just memorize the short sentence in its entirety.

This is the opposite of what audiences expect from someone reading a speech. You've just tripled your eye contact. How could you be reading a speech if every time you open your mouth to start a new sentence and end a sentence you are looking right into the eyes of the people in the audience?

This is UP down UP instead of down UP down. UP is better. The more you are UP the better you will do.

Stand up straight. Keep your chin and your head up. Let your eyes do all the work. Look down to scoop up words. Keep talking when your eyes hit the page. Read the middle of the sentence before you look back up and finish the sentence.

If you need special reading glasses in spite of the large type, don't worry. You can tilt your head forward just enough to catch the text without doing any real damage.

Short sentences are easy. You just memorize the whole sentence (like trying to remember a phone number, you typically have about seven seconds before you start to forget).

Long sentences may be a little tougher. But not to worry—just pop up and down a couple of times in the middle of any sentence of, say, five or six lines.

While you are at it, don't forget to look around the room at the people you are trying to reach. Watch any politician (take the Clintons, or Barack Obama for example). Politicians know that every time they appear to be looking at someone directly, they make the experience personal, even intimate, and gain one more vote. That's hundreds of votes in a sizable audience. By contrast, the person who correctly executes this drill we are talking about here, but fails to embrace the entire audience, comes across as not so likeable or convincing—even though they may be mechanically correct!

The skilled business "presenter" will borrow the Clinton/Obama proven successful approach to command the board room, conference room, or auditorium stage.

Repeat this UP down UP process 100 times and nobody will know you are reading. You may look like you are checking notes, but you will not look like you are reading. If you want to get past the mind and into the heart of your audience (into that primal gut zone where we subconsciously make most of our important decisions) you can't afford to look like you are reading.

The cardinal rule is not to cheat. Don't start talking until you are looking straight into someone's face. Don't rush back down before you finish the sentence so see what the next sentence is.

The only way to know whether you are cheating is to practice a few times in front of a mirror. If you can't see your eyes when you start speaking you are doing something wrong. The same when you finish the sentence.

The more you practice, the easier and smoother it gets. When you are familiar with the words, it gets even easier.

Now, you may start thinking this new skill not only feels weird, but takes too long. That's a common and predictable reaction. Well, it is taking a little longer—and THIS IS GOOD. Why? Because if you are not a professional speaker you may not understand the value of pauses. If you are an amateur, the adrenalin that often kicks in makes time seem to pass more slowly, and pauses feel terrible. This is a normal function of flight or fight—not unlike what you might feel if you were on the highway and about to smash into another car. Your immediate reality may suddenly wind down to slow motion—the brain giving the body time to save its own life.

Let's call this the perception of time gap.

What you don't know is that from the audience's perspective you sound just fine and you are just being yourself—because the audience is on real time.

So if it feels bad, chances are it probably looks good.

In this altered perception of reality, you may find yourself urgently wanting to speak faster. But try to resist the temptation to rush. You may even not take time to breathe properly (it's important to remember to breath normally, and give yourself plenty of air to make sure your voice doesn't fade or fall back in on itself).

If you rush, the result is that you run off at the mouth, start racing through the words, sound like you are reading a speech, and appear to be in a hurry to get it over with (which you probably are). You are so gripped by speed that your eyes hardly seem to come up off the page at all. Before long, you have lost any hope of connecting with your audience. It is clear you are reading a speech—maybe a speech written for you by somebody else.

At this point, you are just another droning sound and people are glancing at their watches.

So we have to create the perception that we are having a conversation—even though we may be reading every word on the page.

That's why we need to do UP down UP instead of down UP down.

Importantly, as I have said, the UP down UP delivery purchases a lot more precious eye contact, and automatically makes it possible for you to appear as if you are engaged in ordinary speech. Translation: you now look more like a leader. You seem to be having an intimate communication with your audience. You come across as thoughtful and articulate. But actually, you are reading.

UP down UP also automatically scatters little pauses throughout. This insures that you have a chance to breathe normally, don't rush, and keep a comfortable pace (necessary for full engagement). All of which helps the audience catch its own breath, relax and absorb the carefully pre-crafted points you want to make.

And the beautiful thing is that if you think you had a bad day, you are still way ahead of the person who read his speech down UP down and thought he had a good day.

The paradox is that this simple routine is in fact just a technique. In that sense, you might be tempted to see it something artificial. But if executed even moderately well, proper execution of a prepared text can make even the most anxious and unpracticed speaker look natural. In life, at a funeral or wedding or birthday celebration, this can mean something. But in business in front of a critical audience it can mean everything.

Now Think About This

If you have gotten this far, you automatically now know more about how to get things done and influence people than 99 percent of your peers and competitors.

You now have the knowledge and skills to lead, drive change, and inspire action—the same knowledge I have been giving CEOs for the last quarter century. With these "secrets" in your hands, you have wisely positioned yourself to out-communicate, out-lead and out-perform in the conference room, boardroom, or on the stage.

I believe that in these few pages you have all the tools you will ever need to forge a better future in ways that may surprise you, and to exceed even your own expectations. This means you are now free to unleash whatever hidden talents and strengths that may been locked, frozen or stifled—simply because they had no means of escape or expression.

The only limit to what you can do now with your business or career is you yourself. So don't get in your own way. Begin using your new knowledge tomorrow and discover for yourself what you may have been missing.

www.ingramcontent.com/pod-product-compliance
Lightning Source LLC
Chambersburg PA
CBHW071256170526
45165CB00003B/1368